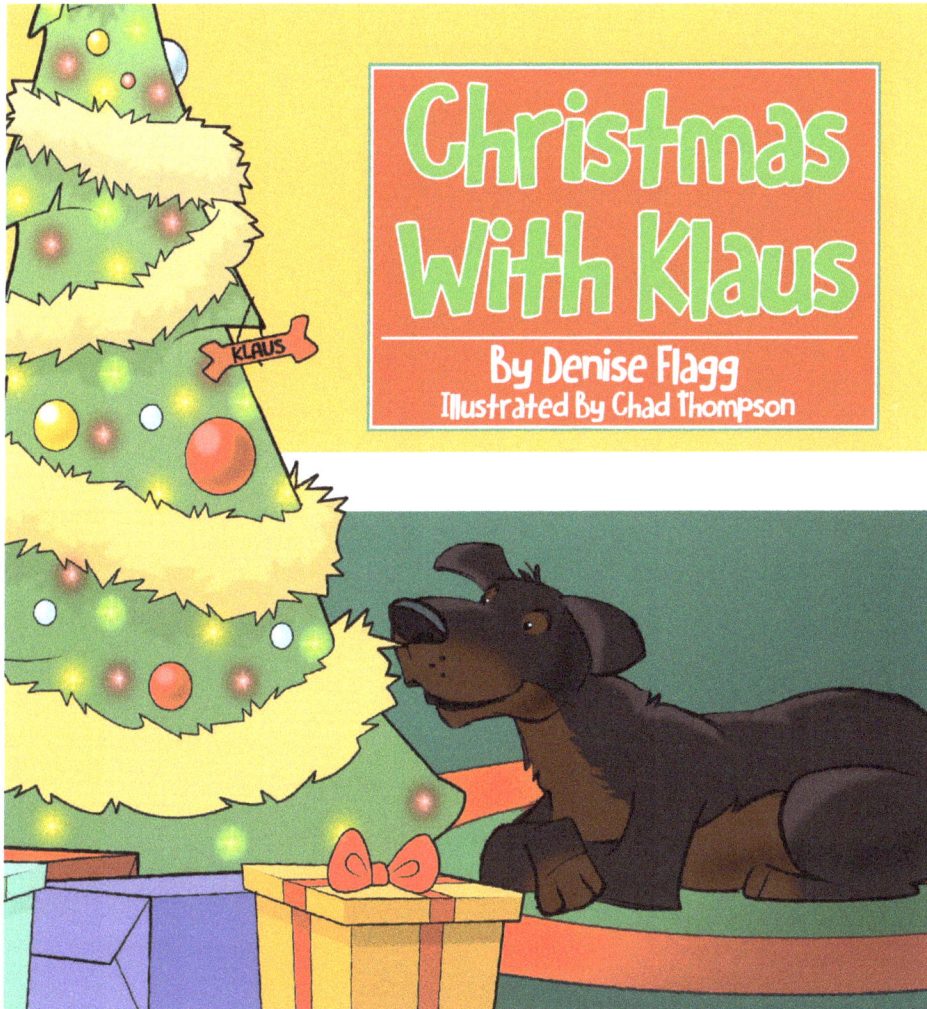

Christmas With Klaus

By Denise Flagg

Illustrated By Chad Thompson

Halo
PUBLISHING
INTERNATIONAL

ISBN 13: 978-1-61244-567-0
Library of Congress Control Number: 2017909434

Printed in the United States of America

Halo Publishing International
1100 NW Loop 410
Suite 700 - 176
San Antonio, Texas 78213
Toll Free 1-877-705-9647
e-mail: contact@halopublishing.com

Words From The Author

Comfy pajamas, hot chocolate, a good book and a dog by my side...
It doesn't get any better than that!

This story was created in memory of our 120-pound, gentle-spirited Rottweiler name Klaus. He was the most human-like dog that we had the joy of loving. In autumn, he loved to play in piles of leaves, and he was always sure to have a snow-covered nose on a snowy winter's day.

Klaus stirred from his nap and blinked his eyes. His family was carrying a **tree** into the house. They set it in a stand and watered it.

"Let's let the tree branches settle a bit before we decorate it."

Klaus sniffed the tree's sharp scent—a Balsam fir. He nudged his owner.

Ernie patted his head. "Did we wake you from your cat nap, Klaus?"

Cat nap? I'm a dog.

Klaus had been curled up in his bed and wanted to stretch his legs, so he went outside for some fresh air. A blanket of snow covered the yard. This was Klaus' first winter. He had never seen snow before. He barked and tried to catch the cold snowflakes on his tongue. After rolling in the snow, his thoughts wandered back to the tree in his house. He was baffled by it, and curiosity got the best of him. He decided to visit his friend, Pebbles. Pebbles was a little older than Klaus, and she always seemed to have the answers to all of his questions.

Klaus woofed hello, when he spotted Pebbles dashing through the snow in her front yard.

"Oh, Klaus, just look at these snowflakes sparkle. Isn't it magical?" she asked dreamily.

"It's so cool." He stuck his nose into the snow and sneezed. "Hey, Pebbles, I have a question for you."

"Klaus, you have such a curious mind. I really like that about you. What's your question?"

"I was wondering if you knew why there's a tree in my house. I've heard of a small house in a tree called a tree house, you know, like a fort for kids. But I've never, ever, heard of a tree in a house."

Pebbles laughed. "You really don't know, do you?" She raced in and out of the bushes, teasing him.

"I haven't a clue. Tell me, please," Klaus chased her.

"It's a Christmas tree," she said happily.

"A Christmas tree? "

"When it's all decorated, it's called a Christmas tree. Did they decorate it yet?" She stopped short. Klaus skidded into her in the soft snow.

"No, not yet."

"Oh, Klaus, I'm so excited for you to see your first Christmas tree, trimmed with twinkling lights and ornaments hanging from its branches. The tree is going to look so festive," she exclaimed.

"Lights? Ornaments? Why?"

"I'll tell you all about it."

Klaus listened, while she explained it to him.

"Christmas is a Christian holiday celebrating Jesus' birthday. Thousands of years ago, a couple named Mary and Joseph had to travel to the city of Bethlehem. You see, the Roman Emperor wanted a count of the number of people living in the Roman Empire, so he ordered everyone to register themselves. When Mary and Joseph arrived in Bethlehem, there was no place for them to stay because the inn was full. Lucky for them, they found shelter in a stable, and that very night, Jesus was born. There was no crib, so they laid baby Jesus in a manger.

"What's a manger?" Klaus asked.

"It's a long, open container that holds water or food for barn animals."

"Oh, I see," said Klaus. "It's kind of like my water bowl."

"Yes, that's right Klaus, but much, much bigger."

"Anyway," she continued, "word spread of Jesus' birth, and Wise Men, following a star known as the Star of Bethlehem, went to visit Jesus. The Wise Men brought gifts with them, and that's why we give and receive gifts at Christmas time to remind us of the gifts given to baby Jesus by the Wise Men."

"We get gifts?" he asked.

"Yes, and we decorate a tree to celebrate the feast of Christmas. Many people place a star at the top of their Christmas tree as a symbol of the Star of Bethlehem, and gifts are placed under the tree. On Christmas morning, we open them."

"That sounds like fun!" exclaimed Klaus. "When is Christmas?"

"December the 25th," she said.

Klaus barked and wagged his tail in delight. Christmas would be here soon.

KLAUS

On Christmas morning, Klaus admired the Christmas tree. He had never seen anything as beautiful before, and the piney scent smelled good. He barked when he saw a Christmas ornament with his name hanging from a tree branch.

Denise and Ernie had placed peanut butter treats and a new chew toy under the tree for him. He tugged off the wrapping paper to uncover his gifts.

Soon after opening his gifts, Klaus spied his friend Sally Squirrel through the den window. She was digging up some of the acorns she had stored away for the winter. He thought about giving her a Christmas gift and wondered what she would like. He remembered seeing a big bag of peanuts on the floor in the kitchen. He found the bag, stuck his head into it and pulled out a mouthful of peanuts. He plopped the nuts into his food bowl. Then, with the bowl in his mouth, he scratched at the back door. Denise and Ernie opened the door for him, peeked out and watched Klaus place his bowl beside Sally Squirrel.

"Hi Sally. Do you know that it's Christmas today?"

"I sure do," she replied.

"I have a Christmas gift for you," he announced.

"Really, a gift for me?"

Using his nose, Klaus nudged the bowl filled with peanuts closer to her and said, "Merry Christmas Sally!"

Sally Squirrel chittered and twitched her fluffy tail. "This is mighty nice of you! Thank you Klaus."

Later, through the window, Klaus watched Sally crack open her peanuts and eat them.

KLAUS

That afternoon, Pebbles and her family came to Klaus' house for Christmas dinner. Klaus wanted to give his friend Pebbles a Christmas gift too and decided to share his peanut butter treats with her.

"These treats are yummy, Klaus. Thanks so much for sharing them!"

"You're welcome," he said, wagging his tail proudly.

"Hey, Pebbles," Klaus said. "I was wondering about something."

"That doesn't surprise me," she said.

"A really weird thing happened the other day. When I woke from my nap, my family called it a *cat nap*. What's up with that? I'm a dog."

Pebbles laughed. "It's just an expression, Klaus. It means a short nap taken during the day. It's called that because cats are known for taking short naps throughout the day."

"Oh, I get it," said Klaus.

"You silly, silly dog."

"Merry Christmas Pebbles!"

"Right back at you Klaus!"

www.ingramcontent.com/pod-product-compliance
Lightning Source LLC
Chambersburg PA
CBHW060800150426
42813CB00058B/2769